Original title:
Deep Sea Dreams

Copyright © 2025 Creative Arts Management OÜ
All rights reserved.

Author: Elliot Harrison
ISBN HARDBACK: 978-1-80587-233-7
ISBN PAPERBACK: 978-1-80587-703-5

## Whispers in the Blue

Bubbles giggle as fish swim by,
A clam with glasses gives a sigh.
Octopus swings with eight left feet,
While seaweed dances to the beat.

A crab in a tuxedo struts around,
On a jellyfish, he found a crown.
Turtles tell jokes in a slow-motion spree,
Underwater laughter, oh what glee!

## Beneath the Surface's Veil

Starfish wearing party hats,
Dance with seahorses, now how 'bout that?
Anemones giggle with colorful glee,
As clownfish joke, "We're the best, you see!"

A whale makes waves, thinks he's so cool,
While minnows scatter, playing pool.
Pearls are disco balls, shining bright,
It's an ocean party, all through the night!

## The Coral Constellation

Coral reefs twinkle like stars at dusk,
With fishy astronauts, it's a must!
Dolphins do flips, with charming flair,
While shrimp form a band, without a care.

Squid in the spotlight, doing a dance,
Laughing at sharks who missed their chance.
In underwater rounds, they compete with style,
Who knew the ocean could be this wild?

## Ghosts of the Sunken Realm

A pirate ghost lost his treasure map,
Now he plays games on an old sunken lap.
Fish play tag with a rusted old sword,
While crabs hold a feast with a banquet aboard.

Mermaids chuckle at silly fish tales,
As octopi juggle with washed-up snails.
The lost ship's crew still knows how to tease,
In a world where laughter floats with ease!

## Voyage into the Unknown

A fish in a hat, sipping tea,
With monocles on, it's quite the spree.
Octopuses dance, they twist and twirl,
Great white sharks wear pearls—oh what a swirl!

The crabs play poker, they shuffle and deal,
While a dolphin juggles a magic eel.
Turtles in tuxedos, they waltz with grace,
Underwater parties, everyone's in place!

## Scale the Underwater Dreamscape

An anchor's lost, it floats like a duck,
Finding a treasure, it's pure dumb luck.
Starfish wear sneakers, all the rage,
Searching for seashells, they start a stage!

Bubblegum squids blow bubbles galore,
While seahorses compete in a dance-off tour.
The seaweed sways in a groovy spin,
Making the mermaids break out in grin!

## The Language of the Fishes

Guppies gossip like fishy chatters,
Shrimp tell tales that really don't matter.
A whale composes a song in the blue,
Jazz hands flapping, oh what a view!

Pufferfish puffing when they feel shy,
Lighting up lanterns, oh how they fly.
The anglerfish winks with a glow in the dark,
Spreading wild rumors, oh what a lark!

**Castaway Fantasies**

A crab in a hammock, taking a nap,
Dreaming of pizza, a crustacean's trap.
Dolphins surf on waves of pure cheese,
While clamsouls chill with a glass of freeze!

Mermaids collect lost sunglasses in style,
Throwing fish fries with a wink and a smile.
Castaways dance with the latest fish trends,
In their underwater party, the fun never ends!

## Veils of the Blue

Bubbles dance like disco balls,
Fish in tuxedos having a ball.
Octopus wearing a silly hat,
Crabs are tapping where the seaweed's at.

Jellyfish float with grace and glee,
Playing tag with the friendly sea spree.
Starfish gossip on the ocean floor,
While seahorses cheer, 'Come back for more!'

## Surrealities Beneath the Tide

A whale sings opera to a school of fish,
While mermaids giggle, granting each wish.
Underwater, laughter bubbles and swirls,
As narwhals dance in a sea of pearls.

Clams throw parties with bright confetti,
And plankton paint nails—oh so pretty!
The conch shell DJ spins with flair,
While dolphins groove without a care.

## Mysterious Harbors of Sleep

Turtles snore in cozy retreats,
While sea cucumbers wiggle their feets.
Anemones fluff their pillows tight,
As hermit crabs join the sleepy night.

Seahorses yawn and stretch their tails,
Drifting off while telling tall tales.
Octopi dream of candy and pies,
In the deep, where the silliest lie.

## **Soul of the Sea**

A fish with a mustache, stylish and bright,
Claims the ocean is a fashion delight.
Octopus models its eight-clenching fins,
While sea turtles give it playful spins.

Squids hold court with a grinning glow,
Reciting poems as the waves flow.
Each shell like a trophy, in laughter steeped,
In the heart of the ocean, where silliness sleeps.

## Currents of the Unconscious

Down where the fish wear hats and ties,
A jellyfish tells jokes that fly.
Octopuses play cards like pros,
While seahorses dance on their tiny toes.

The crabs create a funky beat,
As turtles groove with flippers neat.
Starfish tell tales of curls and bends,
While the reef hosts parties, making friends.

## **Tidal Reverie**

A whale took up a boogie board,
Sliding past a shark who just snored.
Clownfish juggle with seaweed rings,
While dolphins try on silly wings.

The current sways like a dance floor,
And sea cucumbers start to roar.
Anemones wiggle, all aglow,
In this swirling, twirling aqua show.

## Enchanted Grotto

In a cave where the glittering crabs arrange,
A treasure chest hides a fishy exchange.
Mermaids giggle with shells in their hair,
As the narwhal winks with flair and care.

The sea turtles share their tales of delight,
Of sneaky squid trying to take flight.
Pearls drop out, rolling with glee,
In this underwater jamboree.

## Chasing the Abyssal Light

The anglerfish hosts a nightlit ball,
With glowworms shining and having a ball.
Squid paint pictures on the dark,
While clams clap shells to make a spark.

Eels do the twist, a slippery race,
And puffers puff up with silly grace.
The ocean giggles, a bubbly joke,
In this whimsical night where dreams provoke.

## Abyssal Elegy

In the depths where the fish wear hats,
  The octopuses juggle like acrobats.
  A crab sings opera with flair and zest,
    While clams in tuxedos take a rest.

A whale pulls pranks with a mighty splash,
  As sea cucumbers dance in a flash.
  A turtle bets on who'll win the race,
But everyone's laughing—what a silly place!

## **Flickers of Light in Oblivion**

In shadows where the glowworms play,
An anglerfish shows off at the end of the day.
With a flick of its lure, it winks and grins,
Making pals with the plankton as the fun begins.

The jellyfish float like balloons in a breeze,
Giggling softly, they twist with such ease.
While a sardine school performs a ballet,
In the darkened waters, they dance and splay.

## Dances of the Bioluminescent

Twinkling stars beneath the waves,
A party of lights that giggle and rave.
The tiny shrimps throw a glittering ball,
While the dolphins come to give an enthralling call.

They slide and they spin, what a sight to see,
Creating a whirlpool of laughter and glee.
The sea stars groove as bubbles do pop,
Under the waves, they just can't stop.

**The Enchanted Reef**

The coral castles hide treasures galore,
While sea horses trot on an underwater floor.
Clownfish in costumes put on a show,
As the anemones wave with a rhythmic flow.

The parrotfish chime in with silly tunes,
Swaying and bouncing beneath the full moons.
Turtles snap photos with smiles so wide,
It's the most whimsical ride in the tide!

## Kraken's Lullaby

In the depths where shadows play,
A kraken hums a tune today.
With a wink and a twist of its arm,
It rocks the fish, keeps them from harm.

Octopus in pajamas tight,
Dances wildly, what a sight!
With eight legs doing a funky jig,
All the fishes cheer, do a little dig!

Eels are giggling, swaying slow,
As jellyfish float with a gentle glow.
Sharks spinning like tops, oh what a scene,
In this underwater sitcom, they reign supreme.

A clam plays maracas, keeping the beat,
While seahorses strut on their dainty feet.
So if you dive to the ocean bold,
You'll find laughter, tales untold.

## **Abyssal Breezes**

Up above, the bubbles fizz,
Underwater, things are quite the whiz.
A whale with a top hat swims in style,
Makes the anglerfish nod and smile.

A turtle drops a disco ball,
As fish gather, they all have a ball.
With a splash and a dance, they twist and spin,
Who knew the ocean had such a grin?

A hermit crab struts in a shiny shell,
Singing operas, it rings like a bell.
The seaweed sways to this curious tune,
Even the starfish join in the swoon.

The current giggles, the waves clap loud,
In this watery kingdom, the critters are proud.
So take a dive and join the cheer,
In the laughter-filled depths, there's nothing to fear!

## Starlit Waters

Under twinkling waves, the fish hold court,
With a clownfish joke, they playfully sport.
A sea cucumber cracks a silly pun,
While dolphins leap, just having some fun.

Sardines swim in a synchronized dance,
While a crab in a cap takes a chance.
Tickling turtles glide with glee,
Making mischief as they always flee.

The moon plays peekaboo with the tide,
While shrimp flash disco lights, oh what a ride!
The currents carry laughter far and wide,
As bubbles of joy pop and collide.

In starlit waters, joy's on the map,
With guffaws and giggles, take a little nap.
For in this realm where the finned ones gleam,
The fun never ends in their bubbly dream.

## A Canvas of Corals

Corals painting in hues of delight,
While seahorses giggle, ready to write.
Anemones wave their arms in cheer,
As fish float by, holding back a sneer.

A pufferfish pulls a goofy face,
While crabs create a raucous race.
The anglerfish grins with a light so bright,
Stealing the show every magical night.

In gardens of coral, they create a scene,
With starry-eyed fish who just can't be mean.
Each splash and swish tells a story so grand,
As the ocean's palette spreads across the sand.

So come for the giggles, the laughter's the key,
In this watery realm, let your spirit be free.
For under the waves where colors unfurl,
Lies a laughter-filled, whimsical world!

**Sunken Treasures**

In a chest of glittering gold,
Turtles dance, so brave and bold.
Fish wear hats, and lobsters strut,
Crabs are playing in a rut.

Jellyfish are hosting tea,
With octopuses, fancy free.
Mermaids giggle, sharing tales,
While sea cucumbers tell their scales.

A pirate parrot lost his way,
In a bubble, he'll happily stay.
Seashells chime a funny tune,
As sharks attempt to sing a rune.

Barnacles form a wacky band,
With starfish clapping on the sand.
In this world of giddy dreams,
Laughter echoes, or so it seems.

**Journey to the Neptune's Hall**

We rode a wave on a floating log,
Met a dancing, singing frog.
He wore a crown made of seaweed,
And led us to a magic feed.

The Neptune Hall was quite the sight,
With fishy disco, oh what a night!
Seahorses twirled in glimmering shoes,
While dolphins rocked to funny blues.

Clams were rapping, trying so hard,
With pearls that glinted like a card.
Every creature joined in the fun,
Delightful mayhem for everyone!

As we swayed to water's sound,
Unicorns galloped all around.
What a quirky place to roam,
In Neptune's hall, we found a home.

## **The Depths Whisper Secrets**

In the depths where bubbles gleam,
Crabs are plotting a silly scheme.
They whisper secrets to the night,
And giggle at the starfish's fright.

Waves of laughter swirl and spin,
As jellybeans swim with a grin.
The eel tells jokes, they're quite absurd,
And plankton giggle, barely heard.

A clam's a poet, or so he claims,
Crafting sonnets with silly names.
His friends all roll, they find it grand,
A funny world at their command.

From the shadows, whispers flow,
Spreading joy like undertow.
In this world where laughter lies,
Beneath the waves, the humor flies.

## **Beneath the Surface: A Silent Story**

Beneath the waves, the tales unfold,
With giggles of fish, both young and old.
Anemones wave, their tentacles wide,
Inviting all to join the tide.

A sea horse wears a snazzy tie.
While squids ink notes to passersby.
Nudibranchs prance, in colors bright,
Spreading laughter in the twilight.

The clowns of the ocean, jellyfish glide,
Waving gently, they take pride.
With playful winks and joyous sways,
They turn the ocean into a phase.

Here silence sings in a merry tone,
With voices heard, yet never known.
A world of fun lies just below,
Where laughter blooms like coral's glow.

## The Coral Cathedrals

In the coral cathedrals, fish wear suits,
With tiny bow ties and shiny boots.
They dance in schools, a wiggly parade,
While crabs critique the fish charade.

Sea urchins gossip with shells as their phones,
Chatting away in their underwater tones.
Anemones giggle, bobbing with glee,
As the octopus paints like a grand marquee.

Starfish having high tea, that's quite the sight,
While jellyfish hover, shimmering light.
A clam bursts open, a joke in its shell,
'Why don't we dive? It's hard to tell!'

So swim through this laughter, it's quite a scene,
Ocean mischief, where silly reigns supreme.
Beneath the waves, let your worries dissolve,
In this whimsical world, watch your troubles evolve.

## **A Tapestry of Turquoise**

A tapestry of turquoise swirls around,
With turtles wearing hats that are quite profound.
They sip on seaweed, talking in rhyme,
And octopuses juggle their tentacles in time.

Seahorses race, wearing goggles for fun,
'Look at me, I'm number one!'
Sardines in sequins flash and dash,
While dolphins do flips with a bubbly splash.

Crabs play the conch as a groovy beat,
While plankton are groovin', can't be beat.
With laughter and bubbles that twinkle and roam,
This underwater world feels just like home.

Coral reefs giggle, a chorus of cheer,
In this fin-tastic party, come join us here!
With sea stars shining as the spotlight's glow,
It's a jolly old dance, come join the show!

## Where the Manta Rays Glide

Where manta rays glide in elegant sweeps,
They wear little bowties and give friendly peeps.
Like flying pancakes, they float with such flair,
Waving at dolphins, 'Hello! We're rare!'

A sea cucumber joins, donning a crown,
'Just look at me, I'm passing down town!'
Clownfish roll in laughter, paint their faces bright,
While sea turtles groove, 'Get down, that's right!'

Shrimp throw confetti; it's a colorful mess,
As the narwhal twirls in a sparkly dress.
'Is it a dance or just a big tease?'
Said the squid with eight limbs, 'I do it with ease!'

So follow the giggles and flow with the tide,
In waters of chuckles, where friends coincide.
Life's a big party beneath waves so wide,
Join in on the fun, let your worries slide!

## **The Heartbeat of the Trenches**

In the trenches so deep, where the shadows play,
Fish hold a rave, it's the thrill of the day.
With glowsticks in fins, they light up the night,
And the deep-sea creatures dance with delight.

A starry-eyed anglerfish joins the groove,
While a grumpy old grouper tries to approve.
'What's that funky beat?' a wise whale inquired,
'Just a little jam to keep us inspired!'

With laughter echoing off the ocean floor,
Turtles bring snacks from their picnic galore.
'Have a seaweed sandwich, or maybe a pie?'
Shrimp throw confetti, oh my, oh my!

The heartbeat of trenches is quirky and bright,
In this underwater carnival, oh what a sight!
So dive with your friends, share a chuckle or two,
In the deep, where the laughter is fresh as the dew!

## Forgotten Realms Underwater

Bubbles rise like silly jokes,
Fish wear hats and dance in cloaks,
A seaweed band plays tunes so loud,
While crabs play poker, feeling proud.

Octopuses juggle, what a sight!
Clownfish painting with pure delight,
A treasure chest full of rubber ducks,
In this realm, luck just runs amok.

Eels tell tales of lost old socks,
Starfish stacking on the docks,
Every seal is rolling with laughter,
Chasing each other, it's the fun they're after.

Hermit crabs with tiny bling,
Shells adorned for the nightly fling,
This underwater world has quite the flair,
Where silly things float without a care.

**Sirens in the Silence**

Mistress fish with shiny scales,
Sing in tunes of belly laughs,
Their jokes are old, but still they shine,
Making waves with every line.

Mermaids giggle, tails all a-flap,
Woven tales from under the map,
A bubble party on a sunken ship,
As kelp keeps swaying to the quip.

Octo-bards strum tales of fright,
While pufferfish scatter with delight,
"We've lost the net, your tuna's grand!"
They jest and jive in happy land.

By coral castles, laughter reigns,
With jiving squids, we break all chains,
In the depths, we sing away,
Where silence speaks in funny play.

## Beneath the Wave's Embrace

Under waves, where laughter glows,
Hermit crabs wear crazy bows,
Shrimp are techies, coding bright,
While sea cucumbers giggle in fright.

Dolphins chasing after rays,
Casting shadows in funny ways,
They crack up jokes, totally insane,
As laughter bubbles from the main.

Starfish share gossip, all the buzz,
"I swear I saw a fish that does!"
They cheer and shout, spin in delight,
In this realm, everything's just right.

Clownfish paint with colors bold,
Mimicking tales from days of old,
A party under the wide expanse,
Where silliness leads the dance!

## Beneath the Surface

Beneath the surface, where giggles dwell,
Fish tell secrets, but not too well,
They yawn so wide, with crumbs of dreams,
As jellyfish float in comic schemes.

Bubbles pop with each laughing swoosh,
Anemones wobble in a goofy push,
Snails compete in the slowest race,
While sea horses trot with a smiling face.

Comical crabs with hats thought neat,
Strut around, tapping their tiny feet,
"We're the coolest, catch our flair."
As fish laugh and swirl in the salty air.

Beneath the waves, a world so bright,
Where humor reigns and shines so light,
This watery realm, a tale so clear,
Filled with giggles, laughter, and cheer.

## Remnants of a Forgotten Wave

In a bubble, fish do laugh,
Chasing crumbs from the ocean's half.
A jellyfish trips on seaweed's cue,
Swaying like a dancer, it's quite the view.

Starfish throw a party, clapping claws,
While seahorses tango, making laws.
An octopus juggles seashells with flair,
"Is it just me, or is it quite rare?"

Crabs in tuxedos stroll in a line,
"Who knew being crusty could feel so fine?"
With sunken treasure chests filled with gold,
They sip on seawater, feeling bold!

Bubbles giggle, tickling their toes,
As anemones boast about their new clothes.
With all this madness beneath the tide,
Who needs land when here's such a ride?

## Ghosts Beneath the Surf

Ghosts of fish swim with a grin,
Telling tales of where they've been.
Mermaids chuckle at a crab's old joke,
While a clam shares wisdom, but never spoke.

"Don't be a guppy, please do stay,"
An old turtle says in a gentle way.
With barnacles tuning a rock band's tune,
All the creatures dance 'neath the glowing moon.

A whale wearing glasses reads the news,
"Guess what? We're winning at oceanic blues!"
As fish take selfies with seaweed's flair,
Yarn-spinning narwhals make a great pair.

"Let's start a trend," a sponge will say,
"Wearing hats made of coral today!"
So ghosts beneath the surf delight,
In underwater fun, all day and night.

## Porcelain Waters

With laughter echoing in porcelain streams,
The octopus dreams up wild schemes.
A clownfish juggles some algae with glee,
While sand dollars dance in jubilee.

"Did you hear? Starfish can do a backflip!"
A crab exclaims with a confident grip.
Turtles giggle, playing tag with a wave,
"Life under here is ever so brave!"

Anemones invite a shrimp to dine,
"Your pinch makes the soup taste just divine!"
They feast on laughter, with currents that twirl,
As a puffer fish joins, starting to swirl.

Through porcelain waters, joys intertwine,
Each ripple a secret, each splash a sign.
Fish with umbrellas chase mischief anew,
In this underwater world, absurd yet true!

## Fragments of Undersea Realities

In the depths, where the sea gives smiles,
Sea cucumbers turn into fashion styles.
With a wink, a dolphin shows off the moves,
As the ocean floor dances in groovy grooves.

An eel in a tux whispers to a ray,
"Have you heard the gossip from yesterday?"
While plankton twirl in a disco light,
The waves are a party, just out of sight!

"Don't get caught in the net!" shouts a fish,
"Or you'll find yourself in quite the dish!"
But even in trouble, they laugh and joke,
For fun in the abyss is no hoax.

With every splash, the tales unveil,
Fragments of nonsense, or so they tell.
As ocean hearts swirl in playful arrays,
Underwater hilarity is here to stay!

## Mysteries of the Abyss

Bubbles dance like disco lights,
While fish wear tiny party tights.
A crab does a jig, oh what a sight,
As an octopus plays a tune at night.

A whale tells jokes that float on by,
With dolphin friends, they laugh and cry.
The seaweed sways like it's in on fun,
Under the waves, the laughs weigh a ton.

Anemones wave in a silly cheer,
As they pull faces, oh so clear.
A starfish grins with five wide smiles,
While jellyfish glide with style for miles.

So take a dip, join in the spree,
Where fish are silly, wild, and free.
In the deep blue, with laughter we'll roam,
In this underwater, giggly home.

## **Sirens Beneath the Waves**

Mermaids giggle with glittery hair,
Singing songs that float in air.
They trade their tales with fishy glee,
While turtles dance like it's a spree.

With shells as hats, they sway and twirl,
As surfboards made of seaweed swirl.
Their laughter echoes through the foam,
In their underwater, magical home.

A crab in a crown, what a sight to see,
Proclaims himself the king of the sea.
With fishes playing random pranks,
They celebrate with silly flanks.

So, let's dive down, join their song,
Where laughter echoes, we all belong.
Amidst the bubbles and salty brine,
The sirens' banter is oh so fine.

# **Echoes from the Ocean Floor**

Whispers from clams, secrets unfold,
As tired old ships share stories bold.
A sponge plays chess with a sleepy snail,
While sea cucumbers tell a tall tale.

Octopuses juggle with clever delight,
While starfish spin under the moonlight.
Crabs laugh hard, their shells start to crack,
As sea anemones dance, no turning back.

Bubble-blowing fish, filled with cheer,
Send ripples of giggles for all to hear.
An old whale hums a jolly tune,
Making sea urchins sway to the moon.

In this realm of playful surprise,
Joy makes a splash and never dies.
So, come lend your ear to their lively score,
With echoes that call from the ocean floor.

## **Lullabies of the Midnight Current**

As the stars twinkle, the sea sings soft,
To sleepy fish who drift aloft.
A dolphin croons a gentle tune,
While plankton sway, beneath the moon.

Shy squids sketch stories in flowing ink,
As sleepy jellyfish nod and blink.
The crabs close in like a quiet band,
With seaweed rocking to the rhythm's hand.

A clownfish dreams in stripes and spots,
While mermaids knit with colorful knots.
The sizzle of sea sounds a warm embrace,
In the midnight current, soft and chaste.

So close your eyes, let the waves unfold,
With lullabies sweet and stories told.
From the depths of dreams, we swim with glee,
In this wondrous world beneath the sea.

## Nautical Nocturne

A fish in a tux, oh what a sight,
Dancing with crabs every Friday night.
Octopus plays the piano with flair,
While jellyfish float without a single care.

Whales gossiping over a cup of tea,
Fins flapping wildly, how silly can they be?
Seagulls wearing hats, quite out of line,
Join the fish party, it's simply divine!

Mermaids cracking jokes, laughter galore,
With shells in their hair, they always want more.
Clams take the stage, auditioning for roles,
In the underwater talent show, they steal our souls!

Bubbles are popping like fireworks bright,
As we dance with the tide through the starry night.
Life under waves, in a wacky routine,
In this nautical ball, we're the ocean's sweet cream!

## **Tranquil Tides of the Unknown**

In the hush of the night where the sea turtles sway,
A crab teaches salsa, and the squid leads the way.
Clownfish with jokes that are quite out of hand,
Telling tales of mermaids, oh isn't it grand?

Starfish are therapists, giving advice,
Saying, 'Take it easy, don't think twice!'
Seahorses tango in outfits so bright,
While dolphins spin tales of their wild flight.

Corals are gossipers, in hues they compete,
Over the best algae, oh isn't that sweet?
The seaweed joins in, with a wiggle and giggle,
As turtles chuckle, letting out a little wiggle.

Here in the azure, everything's bright,
With all of these antics, the mood feels just right.
So come join the fun, leave your worries ashore,
In the oceans below, we forever explore!

## Stardust in the Ocean's Heart

A starfish with dreams of a rockstar fame,
Picks up a guitar, starts playing the game.
With shrimp backup dancers, they shimmy and slide,
As star dust settles, the ocean's their ride.

Flounders are floundering, trying to dance,
While the eels do the twist, seizing their chance.
With bubbles for microphones, they sing out loud,
Even the waves join in, oh what a crowd!

The currents are buzzing with beats so divine,
As the pufferfish joins in with a twist and a twine.
A sea cow judges, making notes with a sigh,
'Keep practicing, friends, and give it a try!'

Under the moonlight, the laughter erupts,
With rhythm and laughter, excitement erupts.
In this ocean of dreams, every creature takes part,
Creating a symphony that warms the sea's heart!

## Secrets of the Darkened Waters

Beneath the waves where the moonlight peeks,
Live squids telling stories, oh, the tales that they seek!
An eel with a secret, a riddle to share,
While the barnacles giggle, not a worry or care.

Deep in the shadows, a crab plays charades,
With a wink and a pinch, he the crowd invades.
Porpoises chuckle at their silly games,
While the plankton glow softly, like bright little flames.

An octopus pranks with his shifting disguise,
Cuddling up close to surprise and surprise.
Life under here is a whimsical spree,
Where secrets are silly, as silly can be!

So come take a dive, join the laughs and the swim,
Where nothing is real, and everything's whim.
In the darkened waters, joy doesn't wane,
With creaturely giggles, you'll never feel pain!

## Ethereal Depths

Bubbles tickle fishy cheeks,
A whale makes silly faces,
The octopus plays peek-a-boo,
While seahorses race in laces.

Starfish build a castle grand,
With jellybeans for the throne,
Clams with crowns of shiny shells,
Laugh while basking all alone.

In the blue, they spin and swirl,
A party that's a silly sight,
Every creature joins the fun,
Dancing under beams of light.

Waves of laughter echo wide,
As crabs bring snacks to share,
A dolphin's joke makes everyone,
Snort bubbles into ocean air.

## Secrets of the Sunken Paradise

Treasures buried with a twist,
Golden coins and pirate socks,
Mermaids join in this mad mist,
Tickling turtles made of rocks.

Anemones play hide and seek,
While clowns fish burp a tune,
A submersible's on a streak,
Chasing fish that dance and swoon.

Whispers float through coral maze,
As starry-eyed fish giggle bright,
Sardines form a merry craze,
In this underwater delight.

With every splash, a new jest lands,
Eels tell tales of slippery pranks,
Witty waves and silly strands,
Fill the ocean's secret banks.

## **Dreaming in Teal Hues**

Under the waves, the fun begins,
With guppy giggles and flippy fins,
Clownfish juggle a seaweed ball,
While a starfish tries not to fall.

Waves of teal and laughter swell,
As sea cucumbers wish you well,
The anglerfish's light a bright jest,
Turns all dinner plans to a fest.

Nautilus holds a silly pose,
As crabs tap dance on their toes,
The ocean floor is quite the stage,
Put on your funny hats, engage!

As tides roll in, the fun won't stop,
With bubbles popping, flip and flop,
Down in the blue, let joy ensue,
In this world painted bright and true.

## The Dance of Bioluminescence

Glowing critters twirl and leap,
In a balmy ocean sweep,
The fish light up like festive stars,
Chasing jellyfish near and far.

A squid in shades of blue so bright,
Tells knock-knock jokes to the night,
The deep is lively, full of cheer,
With a disco party, let's all cheer!

Barnacles boogie on a rock,
While shrimps wear socks that tick tock,
A whale tunes up with a deep bass,
Making waves in this fun space.

As the ocean glimmers all around,
Every creature can be found,
Dancing joyfully, they perform,
In the magic of their glowing swarm.

## Fantasies of a Seaweed Forest

In a forest made of green,
The fish wear hats like kings.
They dance and prance 'neath bubble trees,
Trying to catch a song that sings.

Stars of jelly, light and bright,
Whisper secrets of the night.
Sea cucumbers play hide and seek,
While crabs just giggle, so unique.

A clam tells jokes, it cracks a grin,
As octopuses juggle with a spin.
Eels in tuxedos make us laugh,
Surveying their wiggly, wavy path.

Bubbles rise like laughter sound,
In this goofy place where joy is found.
With seaweed sprouting wacky hats,
The ocean sparkles, oh so chitchat!

## The Lost Lyric of the Waves

The waves croon tunes that tickle the ear,
While dolphins duet and bring good cheer.
A mermaid's hiccup, a whale's high note,
This concert of gurgles, how we gloat!

Pufferfish puff in a comical way,
Blowing up with each salty spray.
A crab with a mic, he starts to rap,
His rhythm's a journey, a funny map.

Seashells whisper, spinning tales galore,
Of fish who dream of being on shore.
With a splash and a swash, they all unite,
For a frolicsome song in the moonlight.

As bubbles burst with a giggle or two,
The ocean's laughter is all around you.
Chasing a melody, week after week,
In this wavy world, we're all just freaks.

## Tides of Imagination

What if crabs wore tiny shoes?
And fish played cards with jelly blues?
The tides would laugh and roll along,
As seashells sang their silly song.

Starfish dressed in dazzling threads,
Do the cha-cha on their beds.
A silly squid loves to draw,
With ink that leaves you in awe.

Fishermen fish for a joke or two,
While sea turtles do a dance that's new.
With waves like laughter, swirling high,
All marine dreams can touch the sky.

Bubbly thoughts come floating past,
From ships of wishes, deep and vast.
Where imagination's tide will sweep,
Into the ocean's arms so deep.

## Undercurrents of the Heart

In the currents, a silly fish,
Wishes to be a star on a dish.
With friends who giggle and make a fuss,
They dream of adventures upon a bus.

A flounder walks on its fins so proud,
Splashing about, attracting a crowd.
The sea serpent hums a catchy reel,
While clams sit grinning, what a deal!

Don't forget the deep, dark fright,
The anglerfish dressed up for the night.
With a lantern shine that makes you jump,
It's just a prank; he'll join the clump!

In hidden caves, with laughter loud,
Fishy cheers from a clownfish crowd.
With every wave and swish and swirl,
Love floats like foam in a joyous whirl.

## Lullaby of the Lost

In the ocean where fish wear hats,
A squid sings softly to sleepy rats.
Bubble-gum jellyfish dance in a row,
Tickling sharks that put on a show.

Starfish giggle, their ticklish feet,
Waltzing around to the ocean's beat.
Crabs play cards with a slippery eel,
Stirring up mischief with an oceanic wheel.

Turtles travel with snorkels on high,
Whispering secrets as bubbles float by.
A whale hums a tune, absurdly grand,
While crustaceans form a rock band.

With starry skies reflecting in blue,
Fish sip their tea, as they chat about you.
In this watery world, laughter takes flight,
A lullaby sung in the moon's soft light.

## The Twilight of the Ocean Floor

At twilight, the sea comes alive with delight,
Where clams tell jokes and the seaweed takes flight.
Octopuses paint with their colorful arms,
Drawing silly faces with all of their charms.

Crabs wear sunglasses, looking so cool,
Playing hopscotch on a big, sandy pool.
Dolphins dive down to join in the fun,
Splashing about, making everyone run.

A narwhal gives rides on its spiral horn,
While sea cucumbers munch on popcorn.
The laughter echoes through currents and waves,
As fish in tuxedos dance in their caves.

In this twilight of giggles, the ocean is bright,
With jellyfish twirling, a whimsical sight.
The floor comes alive, with legends untold,
In a playful ballet, where joy is sold.

## Oceanic Echoes

Echoes of laughter bounce off the shells,
As fish share stories of their underwater swells.
A snail recites poetry quite in a hurry,
While plankton giggles, not caring for worry.

A friendly shark offers a latte so fine,
With seaweed sprinkles, a breakfast divine.
Seahorses line up for a wild roller coaster,
Zooming through corals, the ocean's own toaster.

The flounders flip pancakes atop their flat backs,
While grinning dolphins plan their next pranks.
Clownfish throw parties with bubbles and cheer,
As whales narrate tales, loud enough to hear.

In this echoing realm, mischief runs wild,
Even sad turtles can't help but be smiled.
The laughter resounds far and near,
In an aquatic circus, there's nothing to fear.

## **Chimeras of the Deep**

In the deep, where silliness reigns without cease,
There be mermaids who giggle and fish who feast.
A three-headed turtle plays chess with a squid,
While sea serpents dance like nobody hid.

Fins wearing hats of various shapes,
Telling tales of old underwater capes.
Starry-eyed otters spinning in glee,
Chasing down dreams in the depths of the sea.

Giant clowns made of coral and shells,
Diving through bubbles, ringing their bells.
A chicken in goggles swims past with a frown,
As octopus jesters wear crowns upside down.

Chimeras of joy twist and twirl all around,
In this quirky kingdom where laughter is found.
Through kelp forests, the silliness gleams,
As creatures rejoice in their wildest dreams.

## The Water's Embrace

In the blue where fish do dance,
A turtle winks, gives me a chance.
Jellyfish float like a balloon,
Say hi to me, then drift away soon.

The crabs throw a party, all in a line,
Clapping their claws, feeling just fine.
A dolphin pops up, cracking a joke,
Splashing all around, oh what a bloke!

An octopus juggles and shows his flair,
While seahorses twirl, like they just don't care.
A giant clam opens with glee,
Inviting us all to a swim and a tea!

With bubbles and laughter, I float on by,
Laughing with fish, oh me, oh my!
In the warmth of the wave, I smile and gleam,
In this funny world, it's all just a dream.

## A Glimpse of the Abyss

Down in the depths where the shadows play,
A grouchy old eel shouts, "Get away!"
I giggle and wave, though he wears a frown,
His fangs look sharp, but his jokes are a clown.

A whale tail splashes, big and grand,
Sending bubbles that pop like a band.
Pufferfish puff, trying to look tough,
But at the end of the day, they're just soft fluff!

As I peek deeper, I see quite the sight,
A sunken ship filled with seaweed delight.
It's home to a crab with a crown on his head,
"Welcome to my palace!" he merrily said.

So down in the gloom where the light's hard to find,
Laughter echoes, so silly and blind.
With a flick and a swirl, I join in their song,
Making mischief in shadows, where I truly belong.

## Chasing Shadows Along the Reef

Along the reef where colors amaze,
I spotted a fish in a sequined glaze.
He twirled and he swam with a wink of his eye,
Said, "Catch me if you can! Oops, I just flew by!"

A starfish called out, "Hey, come and play!"
"I can't walk fast, but I'll sway all day!"
With every little wave, we danced on the floor,
Making fun of sea urchins, who just wanted more.

A needlefish darted, quick as a flash,
Swam in circles as if making a splash.
"I'll teach you to shimmy and get in the groove,
Just follow my lead, let your worries remove!"

With laughter and splashes, we twirled in delight,
Lost in the colors, everything felt light.
In the playful waters, where shadows might creep,
We spun till we tumbled, then fell into sleep.

## The Ocean's Secret Dreams

In the hush of the waves, things start to buzz,
A clam shares gossip, just like it does.
"Did you hear about the fish with a hat?"
"Oh yes, he's a star, he didn't know that!"

Anemones sway in a raucous dance,
While sea turtles munch, not missing their chance.
They giggle and chatter in the salty air,
Judging the snails for moving too slow, with a glare!

A pirate ship lurks with treasures untold,
But the fish just laugh, too bold to be sold.
They hide all the gold in seaweed so bright,
A secret that sparkles, a shimmering night.

As I float near the wreck, I hear tales anew,
Of adventures so wild, made for me and you.
In the depths of the blue, where laughter streams,
Lies the truth of it all—it's the ocean's sweet dreams.

## **Murmurs of the Distant Blue**

In waters wide, a fish with flair,
He wore a hat, said 'Life's a dare!'
He danced in bubbles, swirled with glee,
And shouted, "Join my underwater spree!"

A crab in shades, he crabs the beat,
With moves that left all fish in heat.
They twirled around a sunken clock,
Who knew that time could swim and rock?

A dolphin's joke, a whale's loud song,
"Why not swim? You can't go wrong!"
They flip and flop, and laugh some more,
While octopuses hold the floor.

With seaweed wigs and jelly laughs,
They host grand parties, take mad selfies.
A world of joy beneath the tides,
Where silliness and fish abide!

## Echoes from the Ocean Floor

An octopus tells jokes so slick,
His eight arms wave, his timing's quick.
He asks, "Why did the clam not share?
Because he was a little shellfish, I swear!"

A walrus in a tux, so dapper,
Loud guffaws as he starts to caper.
He slips on seaweed, takes a dive,
And all the fish burst out alive!

The sea cucumbers roll their eyes,
While starfish snicker under the skies.
They plan a prank on the passing tulip,
And all the fish laugh at their schmooze trip.

Then the tide sweeps in, and it's a blast,
Echoing giggles from the deep, so vast.
A party where sea creatures gleam,
In the funny currents of a salty dream.

## Twilight of the Coral Realm

In twilight hues, the reef awakes,
Where clownfish plot and mischief makes.
A seahorse prances, quite the sight,
"Is that my tail, or just the night?"

The corals hum a silly tune,
While jellyfish pop like balloons.
A lobster with a sailor's cap,
Sings shanties, giving the sharks a clap.

"Why don't we ever play hide and seek?
Because the ocean is just too sleek!"
They giggle, roll, and flip around,
Creating laughter commonplace and profound.

A hermit crab sums up the cheer,
Saying, "Every friend is precious here!"
With every splash, a new tale blooms,
In the coral realm, where laughter looms.

## The Siren's Lament

Beneath the waves where mermaids sing,
One lady's tune is quite the thing.
She strums a ukulele, not a harp,
And cracks up fish with her off-key sharp.

"Oh, sailors, please don't take the bait,
For I offer snacks that can't wait!
With popcorn shells and grape seaweed,
Some giggles swim past on this funny feed."

A squid throws confetti, what a sight!
While turtles shrug, they join the fight.
"Let's start a dance, oh what a whirl!
A siren's jest is quite the pearl!"

With waves of laughter, curls aloft,
The ocean's heart beats a little soft.
In funny chorus, they find their way,
As the siren laughs, night turns to day.

## The Endless Blue Reverie

Bubbles laugh and dance around,
As jellyfish wear capes, so proud.
An octopus juggles shells of gold,
While fish tell jokes, quite bold.

Mermaids sip on salty tea,
Their laughter echoes, full of glee.
A crab performs a silly cha-cha,
While clams provide the maraca.

A seahorse twirls with graceful ease,
As starfish chill in the warm sea breeze.
Dolphins play tag with a splashy grin,
Waving hello to the guppy kin.

In this party beneath the waves,
Life's a riot, where all are braves.
The ocean's heart beats with delight,
In its vibrant, whimsical light.

## Currents of Forgotten Tales

In the depths where shadows linger,
Lies a fish that plays the singer.
With a twirl of fins and silly voice,
He makes the seaweed dance by choice.

A turtle spins in a slow-motion race,
While clownfish paint their fins with grace.
Each wave tells tales from long ago,
Of squid that tried to put on a show.

The barnacles tap their tiny feet,
As sea cucumbers offer a beat.
They chant of sailors and ships that roam,
In this underwater, joyful home.

The lighthouse glows with a hearty chuckle,
As crabs gather for a friendly huddle.
Each ripple sings with laughter's might,
In the currents of the ocean's light.

## The Siren's Call to Slumber

Listen closely to the wave's soft hum,
Where sleepy sharks in pajamas come.
A siren croons a lullaby sweet,
While otters gather for a cozy seat.

With pillows made of coral and foam,
They dream of treasures far from home.
A starfish snuggles in with a sigh,
As krill form clouds that float by.

Waves tickle fish in mid-snooze,
While crabs wear nightcaps, snoozing blues.
The moon peeks through, a giggling sight,
As waves sway gently, goodnight, goodnight.

Deep in slumber, the ocean beams,
With underwater antics in their dreams.
A world where giggles softly muffle,
In the siren's gentle, sleepy shuffle.

## In the Embrace of the Deep

In the embrace of the gentle tide,
Clownfish prance with silly pride.
The shimmer of shells, a disco ball,
As crabs proudly do the crab crawl.

Anemones wave like funky dancers,
While fish spin tales of their bold advances.
The eel sneaks in with a nod and a wink,
Suggesting games that make you think.

A chorus of bubbles sings soft and bright,
Echoing giggles throughout the night.
While mollusks trade their secret tricks,
The dolphin crew performs their flicks.

Together under the waves' warm glow,
They celebrate life with a splish and a show.
In this world where joy runs deep,
They hold their laughter and secrets to keep.

## Rafting on the Moonlit Waves

Under the stars, we paddle slow,
With moonlit smiles, we steal the show.
A jellyfish waltzes, with arms so grand,
While seagulls giggle, unbanned and unplanned.

We toast with coconuts, the party's begun,
A starfish DJ, spinning tunes just for fun.
Mermaids in tutus join in the cheer,
Their laughter bubbles, why not bring a deer?

Turtles in tuxedos glide by with grace,
While crabs do the cha-cha, at a peculiar pace.
The waves are our friends, they dance and embrace,
As we raft through the night, in this whimsical place.

So let's row on out, to the rhythm we find,
With the ocean as our stage, it's one of a kind.
Forget all the worries, leave them ashore,
For tonight we're the legends, that the ocean will adore!

## Whalesong in Quietude

The whales hum a tune, that tickles our ears,
A rhapsody crafted through laughter and tears.
They trumpet and giggle, in bubbles and foam,
With melodies sweet, they give us a home.

In this underwater concert, we tap our feet,
As the fish form a chorus, all lively and neat.
Floating along, with our dreams in a whirl,
A sea cucumber tries to twirl and unfurl.

Octopuses juggling, with pies full of zest,
While crabs throw confetti, it's quite the fest!
Anemones sway, like they're shaking their hair,
We join in the jest, without a single care.

So sing with the whales, let your voice rise high,
In this water-bound world, we'll dance till we fly.
Laughing and splashing, till the stars reappear,
With the ocean's sweet humor, we banish all fear!

## The Submerged Symphony

A clam plays the trumpet, a crab on snare,
With dolphins on flutes, they make quite a pair.
A seaweed conductor, waving along,
With kelp as the violins, humming a song.

Tangled in laughter, the fish start to sway,
Boogie-woogie rhythms, make their day.
The octopus, giggling, tosses confetti,
While a shrimp in a bow tie calls for the ready!

The drums of the sea pulse, it's a musical quest,
A symphony written, of jest and of jest.
With bubbles as notes, and currents the beat,
The ocean's great orchestra, can't be beat!

When the concert concludes, there's a thunderous cheer,
As the fish throw a party, with snacks we hold dear.
So dance till the morning, under shimmering light,
In this world made of water, it's pure delight!

## The Ocean's Velvet Veil

Beneath the surface, where secrets reside,
An octopus whispers, with nothing to hide.
In soft velvet currents, we twirl with the flow,
Dodging shy seahorses, putting on a show.

The starfish play poker, but they never bluff,
Their games are quite silly, and always so tough.
Eels form a line, for the conch-shells' song,
While sea cucumbers hum, 'What could go wrong?'

Sardines in a tango, a slippery dance,
They twist and they turn, caught up in a trance.
With humor and charm, they splash in the tide,
Making waves of laughter, that gurgle and glide.

So let us dive deep, beneath the kind sea,
Where smiles are plenty, and laughter runs free.
In this velvety world, with joy we prevail,
For the ocean has stories, behind every veil!

## Elixirs of the Ocean's Depths

In a clam shell bar, they serve fishy drinks,
With jellyfish umbrellas and seaweed blinks.
Octopus bartenders, they twist and they swirl,
Pouring bubble gum cocktails that make the guests twirl.

A whale ordered pie, made of sea foam and sand,
While shrimp in tuxedos did the conga, so grand.
The squids played the sax, with a slick, slimy flair,
Dancing with dolphins, without any care.

Mermaids in wedges, they try to keep cool,
With coral confetti, they break all the rules.
A crab wearing shades, he's the life of the show,
While jellybeans float where the little fish go.

In laughter and bubbles, the ocean does cheer,
With silliness swimming through every blue sphere.
To drink is a giggle, to dance is a dream,
In a world full of joy, with a sea-salty beam.

## Whispers of the Abyss

In the murky depths, where the critters converse,
A clam says a joke, oh, it might be perverse!
A gossipy dolphin, he splashes with glee,
Sharing tales of a shark that likes sipping sweet tea.

A fish with a tie claims he's quite the big deal,
But his jokes flounder more than a poor meal.
With laughter like bubbles escaping the fray,
The octopus giggles, as ink stains the bay.

A seal on a surfboard is riding the wave,
While a turtle in shades, he's just trying to rave.
They dance with the kelp, in a whirl of delight,
Spinning stories and puns 'til they fade into night.

So let's dive into tales of the silly and strange,
Where fish wear tuxedos, and friendships can change.
The whispers of ocean, so funny and bright,
Bring smiles to the surface, from morning to night.

## Beneath the Tides

Beneath the tides, where the giggles reside,
Anemones chuckle, with no place to hide.
A sea snail named Gary, in a race with a wave,
Tells everyone there, he's really quite brave!

The starfish applaud with their many small hands,
As a crab plays the spoons, and a shrimp makes bands.
The clownfish are juggling, a curious sight,
While a group of sea urchins cheer with delight.

An eel with a wig is performing a show,
While plankton toss popcorn, an edible row.
The octopus dances with two left feet,
As the current carries laughter, a bubbly sweet treat.

In this underwater bazaar, the fun never ends,
With high-fives from turtles and new fishy friends.
So if you dare dive beneath where they play,
You'll find smiles and giggles in a warm ocean sway.

## Luminous Shadows

In shadows that sparkle, the fish have a ball,
They twirl through the night, as the sea creatures call.
A firefly squid dresses in lights just for fun,
While a jolly old turtle tells puns one by one.

A manta ray spins like a disco delight,
With a jellyfish glow that's dazzling bright.
The anglerfish wink, with their lanterns aglow,
They joke that they're here for the "dance-off" show.

A clown fish breaks out in a mesmerizing jig,
With a kraken in the corner, who thinks he can dig.
With swirls and with twirls, all the sea creatures play,
In luminous shadows, they dance night and day.

So come take a peek in this world full of cheer,
Where laughter bubbles up, and joy draws you near.
In shadows that shimmer, fun reigns without end,
As the ocean whispers, "Come join us, my friend!"

## Dances in the Deep

Fish wear shoes and polka dots,
As jellyfish groove in tangled knots.
The octopus leads with flair so bold,
Spinning tales that never get old.

Crabs do the cha-cha on the sand,
While seaweed sways as it's hand in hand.
The seahorses twirl, not a care in sight,
Laughing and prancing in pure delight.

Dolphins jump high, with a flip and a splash,
Making big waves while they dash and clash.
They giggle and squeak in the sun's warm ray,
Inviting all fish to join in the play.

So come join the fun in this watery ball,
Where laughter is king, and we all have a ball.
With scales shining bright and hearts all aglow,
Dancing in rhythms that only fish know.

## Depths that Hold Time

In the depths where the ticking goes slow,
Eels wear clocks, and they're never late, you know!
Turtles on roller skates glide with finesse,
While fish play checkers in a seaweed dress.

A crab with a monocle claims he's the best,
Waging bets with a goldfish who's taking a rest.
The bubbles rise slowly, but time flies fast,
In this underwater world, where moments are cast.

A snail on a skateboard says 'Who's won the race?'
While starfish spin tales at a leisurely pace.
And the anemones giggle as the light starts to fade,
Creating a party where no one is paid.

As the seaweed hangs low, and the currents all swirl,
Time's just a concept in this bubbly whirl.
So join in the fun, let your worries all go,
In the depths that hold time, let's steal the show!

www.ingramcontent.com/pod-product-compliance
Lightning Source LLC
Chambersburg PA
CBHW070321120526
44590CB00017B/2773